The Small G

Cover photograph
A traditional wooden greenhouse and cold frame.

Overleaf
Passiflora caerulea.
Both photographs by Michael Warren

The Small Greenhouse

A Wisley handbook

Deenagh Goold-Adams

Cassell Ltd
The Royal Horticultural Society

Cassell Ltd.
1 Vincent Square
London, SW1P 2PN
for the Royal Horticultural Society

First published 1974
New edition, fully revised and reset 1985
                    second impression June 1986

British Library Cataloguing in Publication Data

Goold-Adams, Deenagh
    The small greenhouse.
    1. Greenhouse gardening
    I. Title
    635'.0483   SB415

ISBN 0-304-31107-3

Acknowledgement: Advice on electricity kindly given by
John Weir

Line drawings by Peter Mennim
Photographs by Holland and Clark (Paul Roberts) and
Michael Warren
Design by Kwan Brenchley

Typeset by Georgia Origination Ltd., Formby
Printed by Erasmus N.V. Ghent, Belgium

Contents

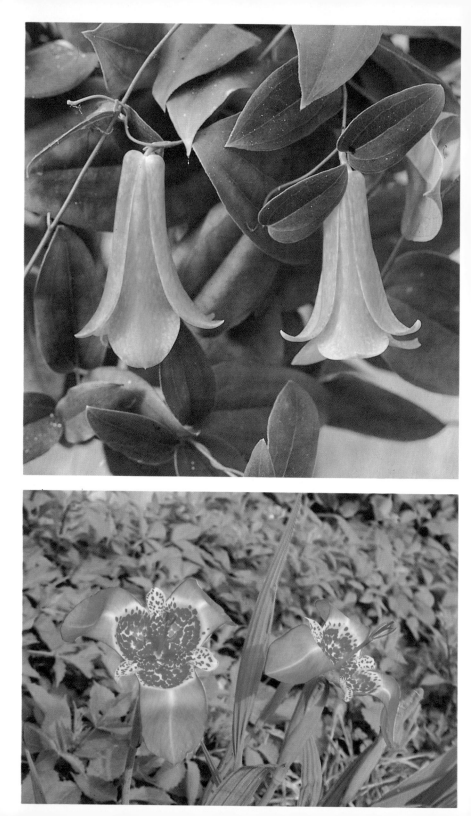

Introduction

There is no mystery in the management of a greenhouse. Regular attention and common sense are the basis of all success under glass, while the application of intelligence, ingenuity or expenditure can overcome most problems even when time or common sense are in short supply! The one essential is a will to grow plants, not just look at them. The key questions are 'Do you want a greenhouse?' and 'Why do you want it?'

The greenhouse must give pleasure and fulfil a role, even if this is one that is not recognised by the neighbours or indeed by the family, let alone by any horticultural expert. A greenhouse is a very personal thing and difficult to share, even if its maintenance does sometimes demand the cooperation of others.

Today the conservatory has become fashionable as well as useful and is another option. A lean-to greenhouse may be used as a conservatory and is often the cheapest way of extending the home.

When it comes to growing plants one cannot ignore personal prejudices. Those who cannot throw anything away will have constant trouble with pots of ailing worn out plants cluttering up the staging. Those who believe that everything they touch will die are probably suffering more from the stresses of an artistic temperament or a disorganised life-style than a lack of horticultural knowledge.

To have a small greenhouse is not one of life's major decisions. It is a fringe benefit that may cost more than some wish to spend on a hobby, but it should not cause any more difficulties than buying a freezer or a washing machine.

The fact that every healthy plant grows bigger every day is an everlasting problem. It is sometimes solved by using the greenhouse as a production unit, or as a staging post for plants that will decorate the garden or the home when full grown. There is always an element of this. Some people are only attracted by rare plants whereas others are equally devoted to familiar flowers. It will be

Opposite, above: *Lapageria rosea*, a beautiful evergreen climbing plant suitable for the cool greenhouse (see page 55).
Opposite, below: *Tigridia pavonia*, an almost hardy bulbous plant suitable for a frost-free greenhouse (see page 54).

found in time that the idea of continuous bloom, so attractive to the beginner, is ultimately as boring as living in a sweet shop. Anticipation is probably the keenest pleasure in growing plants, and the increasing skill and knowledge that can be gathered through life is perhaps the greatest satisfaction. Seed sowing and propagation are essential to a lasting interest in a greenhouse and make this form of gardening a good and inexpensive hobby in experienced old age.

As far as pot plants are concerned the greenhouse can be a nursery, a forcing house, a display centre or, alas, a casualty ward and convalescent home. The more knowledgeable and enthusiastic one becomes, the harder it is to limit and rationalise the use of glass; and this often leads to there being not one small greenhouse but two or three, when one large one would have been so much easier to manage.

It is a sound idea to start with a mixed collection. In fact it is almost unavoidable; there are many plants so prodigal of seed or easily rooted cuttings that they pass from hand to hand and turn up in most collections.

Although it may seem less than friendly to look a gift-horse in the mouth, it is madness not to examine a gift plant extremely closely before adding it to your collection. A hand lens is helpful for identifying pests, and the tender growing points and the backs of the leaves are the places to look. In any case two weeks isolation is a wise precaution with spraying and fumigation as possible alternatives. In a mixed greenhouse or conservatory one hopes to avoid a serious build-up of the pests that are attracted by any one plant family. There is also more scope for a continuous rather than seasonal display. Much depends on the artistic arrangement and this is an incredibly neglected subject.

The true plantsman who sees each plant individually may not be concerned with the general display at all. The only consideration will be the choice of position of light, shade, warmth and air to suit each treasure best. For there is quite a divergence of microclimates even in small greenhouses. Unhappy plants are worth moving and there should also be no hesitation in examining the roots. It does no harm to knock a plant cleanly out of its pot and replace it, and much can be learnt.

In the very limited space of the small greenhouse or conservatory there is no room to grow a large number of plants perfectly. Indeed half a dozen exhibition plants might fill it. There are ways of overcoming this difficulty to suit different temperaments. One is the use of hanging baskets, pots and shelves to create layers of growth.

Another is to concentrate on the 'mini' plant. These have

greatly multiplied in recent times, as the need to transport flowering plants by road in cardboard containers hastened the development of compact strains of the most popular plants. Calceolarias, cinerarias, cyclamen, chrysanthemums, gloxinias, saintpaulias and pelargoniums are just some of those that have been induced to concentrate their charms, and together they cover every season. Other plants are naturally small or propagated yearly from small pieces. The enormous and enduring popularity of fuchsias, chrysanthemums and pelargoniums is partly due to the fact that, as they become unmanageably large, the old plants are replaced by young cuttings taking up much less room.

Another way of saving space is to confine everything to pots too small for full development. With careful feeding this can be remarkably successful but it does not suit either every plant or every person. Some of us wish to grow the best and discard those that do not meet our high standards.

All greenhouses are much the same in summer, depending only on the management of ventilation, humidity and shading for their differing climates. The key questions for year-long interest are what plants can be over-wintered and how early in the year active growth starts. Many plants have a natural rest at a much lower temperature than for their normal growth, while some, like fuchsias, will either rest or grow according to the temperature. Others will grow in winter and rest in summer if given suitable conditions. Many greenhouse plants come from the southern hemisphere and some can be persuaded that a dry rest in our winter corresponds to the summer drought of their homeland.

The final choice of what to grow will depend on the temperature that is maintained in winter. Without any heat at all the scope for an all-the-year round display is limited by the fact that a plant that is not frost-resistant cannot be guaranteed to survive. All the same a lean-to against a south wall can be very rewarding, and spring comes much earlier under any form of glass.

The so-called 'cold' greenhouse sometimes means one with sufficient heating to exclude frost at all times. This creates something like a good Mediterranean climate, depending on the skill of the cultivator. Many tender plants can be grown if kept rather dry in winter.

If a minimum winter temperature between 4 °C (40 °F) and 10 °C (50 °F) is assured, the greenhouse is usually called 'cool'. In any case this is the most popular form of heated greenhouse, even though some prefer the word 'temperate' and set their thermostats around 7 °C (45 °C). All such greenhouses become easier to manage in winter with every extra degree of heat, although the virtual doubling of the cost of fuel with every extra five degrees (F) is a powerful deterrent.

Traditionally the cool greenhouse became 'intermediate' when the minimum temperature maintained was 13°C (55°F), but today 'warm' seems a more suitable term and the only question is the definition of warmth. There is a tendency for warmth to begin at 10°C (50°F) in rather the same spirit that life begins at 40! In other words hope springs eternal and some tropical plants will survive although they are happier at 13°C (55°F). This last temperature is the highest that amateurs generally aim at in the free-standing greenhouse. Where there is a conservatory against a house wall connected with the central heating system higher temperatures may prevail and the tropical plants we call house plants can be freely grown.

For those who prefer to specialise, a wide range of bulbous and alpine plants can be grown in the cool greenhouse.

Top left: *Streptocarpus* come in a wide range of colours; this is the hybrid 'Tina' (see page 57).

Top right: African violets (*Saintpaulia*) are amongst the most popular of houseplants, and are easily grown from cuttings.

Below left: Gloxinias (*Sinningia*) are some of the best known of the gesneriad family (see page 57).

Below right: *Hippeastrum* 'Apple Blossom', a spectacular bulbous plant suitable for the warm greenhouse (see page 54).

Site and structure

An amateur greenhouse of up to 1000 cubic feet does not usually interest either the planning or rating authorities, unless it is on a boundary or attached to a building. The local building inspector will have to approve any structure being added to a house and there are regulations about size and use so that it is advisable to check the position locally. If you are a tenant, remember that once fixed to a permanent concrete or brick base, the greenhouse is no longer a tenant's fixture.

Some greenhouses are erected directly on the ground while others have portable base plates of concrete, wood or metal. A really solid base does add to the life of the structure and it is obvious that, if in time the building sags, the glass is likely to crack and leaks will develop. The glass needs to be set in some soft material (putty is no longer used) to avoid leaks and loss of heat in winter.

The materials of which greenhouses are made vary in popularity as their cost and ease of maintenance increase or decrease. It is never difficult to find a possible scientific advantage for either a new or cheaper material. Yet everyone has a preference for wood or metal, regardless of its intrinsic merit, and it is a pity to spend one's leisure in a building one instinctively dislikes.

In some settings the traditional white painted softwood is so much more visually satisfying that it must be preferred for a conservatory. Nevertheless the cost of frequent painting needs to be faced. The glazing bars of even a wooden conservatory will probably be of aluminium today.

The most popular wood, known as western red cedar, is a rot-resisting softwood from North America. This wood from the tree *Thuya plicata*, is usually stained with a solution to make it waterproof and retain the natural red colour. Another method of keeping the wood in good condition is a yearly treatment with thick penetrating oil.

The aluminium alloy greenhouses so popular today need less maintenance than wood, but vary greatly in quality both in design and strength. They can also be had in anodised colour which can have a bronzed appearance or white vinyl covered aluminium.

On a windy site one needs to choose a greenhouse of sound construction fixed to a solid base.

Although metal is colder than wood this is not of serious consequence in small lightly constructed buildings. Wood is more convenient when it comes to fixing up shading material or a plastic lining. Maximum light in winter is vital, but this is affected more by the position of the greenhouse than its construction nowadays. An east-west orientation is best for winter light but in a very small building this does not make much difference. Galvanised steel is another possible construction material. This is more rigid than aluminium alloy, but will need regular painting as galvanizing is not a permanent protection.

A lean-to built against a wall saves a great deal of fuel in winter; but it receives less light and is more difficult to ventilate efficiently than the ordinary span-roofed type. A good choice in certain circumstances is a three-quarter span. This over-tops a wall and has two-way ridge ventilation but is an expensive option as it has to be custom-built. A south wall is regarded as the best position, though very hot in summer. Nevertheless, a lean-to on any wall is possible and often a joy, if the plants are chosen for the light available. Sometimes the layout or lack of space makes a round or hexagonal greenhouse the best choice.

If a greenhouse is on a solid base, it is less suitable for growing plants in the ground. Brick walls up to the staging save fuel, but are now rare because of the cost of the brickwork. A substantial wooden base is some substitute, but plastic panels do not save fuel unless thick insulating material is fitted inside them. As many additional plants can be grown under the staging when there is glass to the ground, a panelled base can be a false economy.

It is not possible to find all the virtues in one ready-made structure, but it is well worth comparing one with another. The Chelsea and Southport flower shows are good places to examine a variety of greenhouses and conservatories. As the available site may affect the choice this needs to be considered first. The distance from a source of electricity is important even if it is not going to be used for heating.

Lighting, fans, seed-raisers, mist propagation and power drills are just some of the many extras using electricity. If natural gas is to be used for heating or if an outside oil tank or fuel store will be needed, this is the time to decide where they will be. Mains water is also helpful, even though rain water is often preferred to tap water. Automatic watering may need mains water pressure or a water tank at least 3 feet (90cm) above the staging.

If plants are to be grown in the ground, the soil must be reasonably well drained and this is more easily attended to before the greenhouse is put up.

Above: A small cedar greenhouse in one of the model gardens at RHS Garden, Wisley.

Below: A small lean-to greenhouse/conservatory.

Interior of a small mixed greenhouse, showing some of the range of plants that can be easily grown by the amateur.

A position that is not overshadowed by trees or buildings and open to winter sunlight is the aim, and one does not want a hedge or fence too close although shelter from wind is important. There is some conflict of opinion as to which way to align the greenhouse, though this may be determined by the site. I favour an east-west alignment which is good for winter light and gives a sunnier and shadier side.

Here are some points to look for when choosing a small greenhouse or conservatory:

1. Method and amount of ventilation and whether it can be automated. Extra ventilation is almost always essential as when the ventilators are open they should equal at least one fifth of the floor area.

2. General stability and likely wind resistance if the site is exposed.

3. Foundations required and method of construction.

4. Strength and height of staging provided and whether it is suitable for your purposes. Much gravel, clay pots or sand capillary benches can be heavy. One needs an absolutely flat surface for all capillary watering.

5. Arrangements for disposing of water from condensation inside the greenhouse.

A newly constructed aluminium greenhouse showing various ventilation systems.

6. Width of entrance.
7. Check terms if manufacturers deliver and erect, and look at 'Do it yourself' building instructions.
8. Make sure glass is included in the price and discover if it will be delivered with the greenhouse.

If a greenhouse is put up on grass, the turf should be removed with an inch of top soil and stacked to make potting soil. However, the busy gardener may feel more inclined to cover the grass with black plastic sheeting until it is dead and then cultivate the soil or remove it for use elsewhere. If plants are grown in the ground, the soil is managed much as in the open garden, bearing in mind that it does not have the benefit of frost or rain. A friable loam containing plenty of organic matter is the aim.

When ground is not cultivated, the floor inside the greenhouse can be treated in various ways. On a wet site concrete is probably the best. For retaining moisture in summer, when the floor is sprayed to increase the humidity, rammed soil or ash with a duck-board path has been the traditional working arrangement. A central path of paving blocks with gravel on the soil under the benches is more attractive. A conservatory often looks best if the same paving as the terrace continues inside or alternatively if the flooring in the house is carried through to the conservatory. This is not always practical. Wall to wall carpeting cannot be 'damped down' and vinyl tiles can be death traps when wet.

The actual foundations of a free-standing greenhouse should rest on firm sub-soil. When laying concrete or brick foundations, leave entry points for electric cables and water pipes. Pieces of hose do well for this, although I once found that a pygmy vole took up residence as a result!

Heating and ventilation

The cost of heating has multiplied so many times in recent years that we hesitate before deciding to heat a greenhouse at all. At the same time the savings made by raising, preserving and propagating our own plants have also greatly increased.

An amateur's collection of plants can be irreplaceable, costly to replace, or almost valueless; so the cost of installing and running truly adequate heating for a severe winter may be either well worth while or quite unacceptable. Every ten years or so there is a winter when low temperatures persist for several weeks and plants will certainly be lost unless the realities are faced.

It is possible to grow only hardy plants or those that become hardy with shelter from our winter rains, but this is not usually the aim. Most of us have a mixture of tender plants and want some to be decorative at all seasons. This is even more true of a conservatory attached to the house. Few plants mind a brief drop in temperature so long as they do not freeze, and daytime power failures rarely cause serious harm.

The cost of heating will vary with the region of the country and the exposure, as well as the elevation of the site and the degree of double-glazing or other insulation. Although many tender plants may be brought safely through mild winters in an unheated glasshouse against a south wall in the warmer parts of the country, one is always at the mercy of the elements without artificial heat. Many people try to nurse tender plants through the winter by lighting a heater on cold nights only. This adds human error to the dangers and can be quite expensive, as it is often done without thermostatic control.

Greenhouses can be heated by natural gas, solid fuel, paraffin, bottled gas or electricity. Their cost also progresses in that order, with electricity the most efficient and expensive unless you are able to benefit from the 'night rate' on a two-rate tariff. This can halve the cost of the night hours.

The major decision about heating is what minimum temperature to maintain in winter. Unfortunately every extra degree of heat tends to make the control of the environment easier and the results more rewarding. A temperature of 4°C (40°F) will exclude frost and is often chosen for a cactus collection, which rests in winter, as well as by many of us on grounds of cost. What is known as the 'cool' greenhouse should not fall below 7°C (45°F)

A group of cacti showing some of the wide range available (see page 57).

and this is the lowest satisfactory temperature for plants that are actually growing in winter. One can preserve them and expand into a splurge of growth in spring so long as frost is excluded, but I think year round happiness and comfort for all concerned are greatly increased at 7°C. To raise the temperature to 10°C (50°F) will double the fuel bill, while the 'intermediate' house at 13°C (55°F) will double it again. The warm greenhouse at 18°C (around 65°F) could cost five times as much as the cool greenhouse.

The daytime temperatures will always be higher than the minimum set, except in very bad weather. Very little artificial heat is used in daylight at the lowest temperatures, but a warm greenhouse needs continuous heating for at least half the year. It is possible to have a thermostat with different day and night temperatures and this is the ideal.

All greenhouse heating systems are rated at a maximum heat output expressed in either kilowatts or British Thermal Units per hour (1kW = 3412 Btu/h). This will be found printed on the equipment or in the instructions and is essential information. One can only make a realistic assessment of the heating needed to maintain a given temperature in a particular greenhouse by making a calculation of the heat-loss of the structure. This is simpler than it looks as the thermal factors of the various materials are known. These are expressed in Watts per square metre per degree Centigrade (W/m² deg C) in the following table and are known as 'U' values.

Thermal transmission co-efficients ('U' values) of materials

	W/m² deg C
Horticultural glass	5.7
500 gauge polythene film	5.7
Wood, 2.5cm	2.6
Wood, 3.8cm	2.4
Brickwork (unplastered) 11.4cm	3.4
Brickwork (unplastered) 22.8cm	2.7
Brickwork (unplastered) 34.2cm	2.1
Concrete, 10cm	4.0
Concrete, 15.2cm	3.6
Earth floor	1.9
Concrete floor	0.7

The following example will show how the calculation is done:

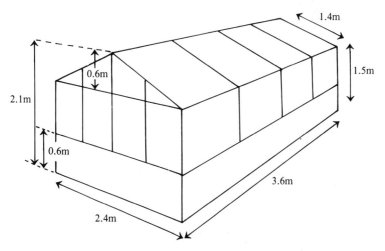

Area of roof (3.6m × 1.4m) × 2 = 10.1m²
Area of glass sides (0.9m × 3.6m) × 2 = 6.5m²
Area of glass ends (0.9m × 2.4m) + (0.6m × 1.2m) × 2 = 5.8m²

Total area of glass = 22.4m²

Heat loss from glass @ 5.7W/m² deg C: 22.4 × 5.7 = 127.7W/deg C
Area of side walls (brick) (3.6m × 0.6m) × 2 = 4.3m²
Area of end walls (brick) (2.4m × 0.6m) × 2 = 2.9m²
Total area of brick walls = 7.2m²
Heat loss from walls @ 3.4W/m² deg C: 7.2 × 3.4 = 24.5W/deg C
Area of floor (soil) 2.4m × 3.6m = 8.6m²
Heat loss through floor @ 1.9W/m² deg C: 8.6 × 1.9 = 16.3W/deg C
Total standing heat loss from greenhouse = 168.5W/deg C (i.e. sum of total heat losses).

Add $\frac{1}{3}$ for air leakage from the structure through joints and cracks etc.

$$168.5 \times 1.3 = 219.1 \, W/\text{deg} \, C$$

To achieve a 14°C temperature life and 7°C minimum winter temperature for this greenhouse a loading of 3067W or 3.067kW is indicated (i.e. 219.1 × 14W or $\dfrac{219 \times 14kW}{1000}$)

For a 20°C lift to maintain, say, 13°C the figures would be 4382W or 4.382kW. Rounding up or down to the nearest 500W one could use 3kW or 4.5kW heaters respectively. In a very cold area one might feel it wise to instal the capacity for a greater temperature lift in severe weather although aiming only at a low minimum temperature.

The running costs of all heating systems depend on the set minimum temperature, and effective thermostatic control is absolutely vital if much electric heating is to be used. The newer electronic thermostats are more accurate and reliable than the mechanical rod type, and both need checking yearly against a mercury thermometer. Thermostats need careful placing so as to reflect conditions among the plants; they should not be in the roof or on the floor. A shady spot away from the door is best. Aspirated thermostats can help with both heating and ventilation control in difficult conditions.

Electricity in your Garden published by the Electricity Council gives guidance on electricity consumption in various parts of the country, and the local electricity board can advise on the most suitable tariff.

The most primitive form of greenhouse heating is the small paraffin burner that depends on frequent filling and wick trimming. This is the favourite emergency standby. Although in good hands this kind of heater has been made to work wonders for decades, it is not suitable for maintaining a reasonable temperature in cold weather. It is sometimes difficult to assess what heating can be given by paraffin heaters, but the makers of the more effective ones do give the number of British thermal units produced per hour by their heaters and also the number of hours the heater will run on one filling. The burning of one gallon of paraffin will produce about 72,000 Btu's and so it is possible to make a rough assessment of the actual temperature one of these heaters can give. One Btu per hour is the equivalent of 0.293 Watts; so one may be trying to heat a greenhouse with something little better than an electric light bulb.

Burning paraffin without an outside flue discharges a considerable amount of water vapour into the atmosphere. Some damaging fumes build up unless a chink of ventilation is always left open. The fact that oil heaters burn on regardless of the temperature has been partly overcome by non-electric thermostats, which reduce the rate of oil consumption as the temperature rises. These are fitted to some of the larger heaters. It is also possible to have a flued paraffin boiler to heat water pipes in a greenhouse.

Natural gas is a relatively new and reliable source of heat that can be used in glasshouses without a flue. The local gas board has to approve the type of heater and how the supply pipe is laid. They may charge very reasonably to do the work but have done little to encourage this use of gas. The gas heaters have a non-electric thermostat and are designed for small greenhouses, so that more than one may be needed. There must be ventilation at all times when gas heaters are burning and, like paraffin, they add moisture and carbon dioxide to the atmosphere. A possible hazard with natural gas is that, if ventilation is inadequate, some plants may be affected by leaf or bud drop or some other side-effect from the substances in the gas, which are similar to the natural ripening agents of those plants.

For a greenhouse needing 8kW or more heating one can have a natural gas heater with an outside flue and electrical controls. This blows warm air either freely or through ducting. Some flue-less gas heaters are designed for use with either natural gas or bottled gas. A bottled gas heater is a useful emergency heater when other fuels fail, but it is expensive and gas bottles do not last for long. Propane is the gas to use as it does not freeze.

In the past the traditional method of heating glasshouses was by means of 4–inch cast-iron water pipes heated by a solid fuel boiler. Today solid fuel is more attractive in the colder north of the country. Fuel is restricted in smokeless zones, but a variety of fuels can be used. In an emergency the only certain fuel is the one stored on the premises. Obviously all boilers need regular attention and maintenance, although the stoking and cleaning have been simplified in recent years. Modern piping can be assembled by the handy man and the system adjusted to any size of greenhouse. Unless the boiler is protected from the weather, it loses much of its efficiency and a fuel store is also needed. However, for the higher temperatures solid fuel is worth considering.

Electricity is undoubtedly the most convenient and adaptable fuel for the small greenhouse. Unfortunately cost may prevent its use, but it should always be considered for frost protection. A fan heater distributes warmth well and avoids installation costs, but a thermostat incorporated in it will not reflect the temperature very accurately where the plants are growing. One always needs a maximum and minimum thermometer to check what is actually happening in various positions. There are always cool and warm spots that one can use to advantage.

Electric tubular heaters distribute the heat well and can be fitted to warm any size and shape of greenhouse. They are banked round the sides of the structure and should be 4 in. (10cm) from the outer walls and at least 8 in. (20cm) above the floor. Space should be allowed for the warm air to rise between the glass walls and the benches on which the plants are growing.

Before leaving electric heating I should mention soil-warming as a most economical way of using electricity in horticulture. Soil-warming cables are laid evenly in parallel lines with gentle curves at the ends, so that the wires never come close to each other and overheat. The most even temperature over the whole surface is achieved when the spaces between the cables are equal to, or less than, the depth at which they are buried. If they are not deeper than the width between them, there will be greater warmth directly over the wires. Screened mains cable controlled by a thermostat is used to achieve a soil temperature between 21°C and 24°C (70°F–75°F) for rooting cuttings and raising seeds. Where only a few plants are wanted a small electric propagator is invaluable.

Electricity in a greenhouse is a tremendous help for so many purposes, but any installation needs, at the very least, checking by a competent electrician in such a damp and potentially dangerous situation. Any exposed cable must be of a suitable kind to withstand sunlight and all installations need looking over regularly.

Whatever form of heating is decided upon the area to be heated needs to be kept as small as possible and some form of insulation used in winter. If the warmth is to be held in, some loss of light is inevitable and there is always a shortage of light in winter. It depends on the plants grown, but with tender shade-loving plants I would have no hesitation in lining the rof as well as the sides of the greenhouse. However, access to the ventilators should always be left. Lining materials tend to attract condensation droplets which obscure the light still further, and the humidity of the greenhouse atmosphere is also increased. Bubble plastics give rather more protection than simple sheeting. It is not impossible to put up a material to give shade in summer and some insulation in winter, but it will not be the best for both purposes. There are meshed materials which shade but give little insulation and double-walled plastics which give more protection from cold but are opaque. Most materials have a limited life in the greenhouse and both they and the glass become obscured if they are left up permanently. Even with the most complete and careful insulation it is unwise to count on more than a 30 to 35 per cent saving of fuel. If either internal or external blinds are used for shading some warmth is conserved by lowering them at night in winter.

It is now possible to have double-glazed glasshouses and this is worth very serious consideration, particularly for conservatories and when a high temperature is going to be maintained.

The key to success under glass is the control of climate (of which heating is only a part) in a way that adjusts to the vagaries of the weather. The aim is always a steady temperature without violent fluctuations and preferably only moderately cooler at night than during the day. It is one of the great virtues of glass that the sun shining on it raises the temperature inside much more quickly than the trapped heat can escape. This saves a great deal of fuel even in the coldest weather, though it does mean that ventilation must respond fairly quickly to weather changes, particularly in the smallest greenhouses where temperature fluctuations are the most rapid. March, April and October are perhaps the most difficult months, as the sunshine can be warm though the outside temperature may be too low for free ventilation when the sun disappears.

For a few people with leisure, who are tied to their homes, it may be a pleasure to keep a constant eye on the weather and wind direction, so that greenhouse ventilation can be adjusted to the best advantage. To most of us this is either impossible or unthinkable. Indeed it can be the reason for rejecting the very idea of a greenhouse.

Although I am not a great believer in extractor fans, they are perfect for saving a closed greenhouse from frizzling up in unexpected sunshine. Often a greenhouse door is left open in warm weather, but must be locked if the owner is out or away. Then, too, a fan can save the plants. Although it is sometimes recommended, I do not regard an extractor fan as a satisfactory substitute for all other forms of ventilation. Proper greenhouse fans have louvres to prevent wind blowing in and should be controlled by thermostat.

Ventilation is measured by air changes per hour, and 30 changes per hour are considered enough for amateurs. As a rough guide on this basis a 228mm fan is said to be sufficient for a volume of up to 14 cubic metres and a 300mm fan up to 28 cubic metres. Professionals are always advised to have at least 60 changes of air per hour – from which you can draw your own conclusions. One of the controlling factors is that in a small greenhouse it is difficult to find a place to fit a large fan. All extractor fans need their thermostatic control set at least 2°C above the temperature of the heating thermostat.

It is believed that greenhouse ventilators should open up an area of not less than one fifth of the floor area. In practice it is usually a good thing to have as much ventilation as can be fitted in small greenhouses. Plants need fresh air for healthy growth, and in summer good ventilation is necessary to keep down the temperature to reasonable levels when the sun is shining. In general all temperatures above 24°C (75°F) are undesirable, though not always avoidable. In winter stagnant cold damp air encourages every sort of mould and rot amongst the plants that are barely growing. Then, ventilation is still needed and artificial heat adds to the occasions when ventilation can safely be given.

At the time of writing, the popular automatic ventilation controls that do not require electricity are activated by a cylinder filled with a composition which expands and contracts according to the temperature. These ingenious devices come in various forms and are adjustable within limits. They are fairly satisfactory in most weather conditions but I like to have at least one adjusted by hand. They are not supposed to operate centrally pivotted ventilators, but with counterweights and ingenuity they can be made to do more than their makers claim. There is also one for louvred ventilators.

Shade is another way of lowering summer temperatures under glass, and if there was perfect ventilation very little would be needed. Shade-loving plants and delicate seedlings may need shading in March, and a high proportion of greenhouse plants benefit from some shading from April until the end of September. It is, of course, only actually wanted when the sun is shining, but it is usual to compromise and create a filtered light that is not too dark on dull days.

It is possible to have automated wooden slatted blinds fitted outside the structure but at great cost. This gives both shade and the maximum cooling effect. Internal roller blinds do not cool the structure in the same way, but are much used and could be automated. Another possibility is internal slatted blinds, the angle of which can be adjusted according to the weather. The simplest arrangement is to use one of the temporary shading materials, which are diluted with water and lightly painted on to the outside of the glass. This can be done progressively as the sun strengthens, starting with a light coating on the south side to protect vulnerable plants in March. These materials can be wiped off at the end of the season. Fine plastic netting designed for greenhouse shading is also effective and has a life of several years.

The other means of combating excessive heat in summer is by increasing the humidity, and this is discussed in the next chapter.

Watering and humidity

Watering in the greenhouse is an essential activity about which there is much disagreement. Some plants prefer a constant moisture, while others are believed to prefer to become rather dry before being watered. In practice the majority will adapt fairly readily to any steady regime that does not keep them sodden or allow them to dry out enough to begin to wilt. It is, however, a golden rule when watering by hand either to give enough water to moisten all the soil in the pot or to refrain from watering at all. Clean rain water (except in very large industrial towns) is likely to be better for the more delicate pot plants and may be essential for lime-hating plants if the mains water is very alkaline. It is also an advantage if water can stand in the greenhouse before use in cold weather to take the chill off. However, tap water coming under pressure is highly charged with oxygen which is beneficial and static tanks easily become polluted. It is not always understood that air penetrates between the soil particles and that it is essential to all but bog plants that it should. If water fills all the air spaces in the soil for long, most plants will suffer root damage.

Every beginner wants to know how often to water in terms of days and this is an unanswerable question. The rate at which the soil in a pot dries out is affected by sunshine, temperature, atmospheric moisture, type of compost, and how firmly it is packed. The nature and size of the plants and whether they are growing or resting are other factors, not to mention the material of which the pot is made. The advantage of hand watering is that it can be selective, and success must be based on observation.

Holidays and other absences from home are the bane of the greenhouse enthusiast, and now that automatic watering is so widely practised commercially every amateur should give it serious thought.

The word automatic is often applied very loosely to some watering aids, which depend on daily attention and merely require less skill and save time when looking after large numbers of plants. It is, of course, easier to explain to a helpful friend or neighbour that a tap should be turned on or a tank re-filled than describe the drinking habits of all the precious plants, but this is not automation!

There are two main types of watering system that can be fully automated. The first is capillary watering, by which pots standing on damp (capillary) matting or sand draw water from below by capillary attraction. The second method is to water the surface of the soil in each pot by means of an individual nozzle or tube. Such trickle and drip systems need electricity if they are to be truly automated, whereas capillary systems need only a source of water.

It is difficult to give simple general advice about automatic watering, because conditions in each greenhouse and the collection of plants grown vary enormously. Even when a watering method is chosen, the interests and aptitudes of the gardener will affect the result, as in all gardening. Temperatures maintained in winter and the method of heating will also alter the climatic conditions in which the watering takes place. Nevertheless, a general understanding of the principles involved and the equipment available is essential, if the best use is to be made of it. Unfortunately all research is done for commercial interests and the equipment offered to the amateur is mostly marketed by very small firms, who are keener to produce something new than a system of lasting benefit.

Those specialising in a single kind of plant or crop are faced with the limited problem of its season of growth and rest, but most amateurs grow a mixed collection of plants in pots as well as raising seedlings in spring.

The average small greenhouse tends to be too hot in summer, poorly ventilated, and with too dry an atmosphere. All forms of automatic watering are likely to improve these conditions, and capillary benches, which add moisture to the air and accommodate the largest number of plants in the smallest area, are particularly suitable.

In winter the problems are different. In many greenhouses a combination of low temperatures with a damp atmosphere and poor air circulation encourages troubles such as botrytis, and unnecessary dampness is to be avoided. As better air circulation is achieved with slatted benches, it would be ideal if each pot stood well clear of its neighbours and was watered individually according to its needs.

In commercial glasshouses plants do well with individual drip watering to well-spaced pots on wiremesh benches. In a small private greenhouse or conservatory space is limited and appearance often cannot be sacrificed to technology.

CAPILLARY WATERING

The capillary bench is in many ways the most easily controlled and satisfactory method of automatic watering. In the early days sand benches were constructed where the pots stood on damp sand which was 2 inches above the water-level (5cm). Commercially this system was not very successful and it never caught on with the general public. In commerce there was too much trouble with the spread of disease. Personally I have used sand benches for fifteen years and prefer them in spite of a certain amount of trouble with worms and moss. The valuable aspect of this system is that each pot plant standing on damp sand absorbs from below, by capillary attraction, only the amount of water it uses. So long as the bench has a controlled and constant water level, sudden changes in the weather and the water needs of the plants are catered for. As there is never a shortage of water, the plants grow steadily and fast.

There is a limit to the height of the pot that can be used when watering by this method. The capillary attraction only carries the water up about 5 in. (12.5cm) when the water level is held 1.5 to 2 in. (5cm) below the surface of the sand, which has been found to be the most satisfactory arrangement for most plants. Pots up to 6 in. (15cm) high are satisfactory on capillary benches; larger pots are better watered from the top. For a really reliable and effective capillary bench, it is necessary for it to be level ($\pm \frac{1}{8}$ inch) and to have a controlled and constant water level. It is possible to cover capillary benches with plastic sheeting with a hole for each pot if one is seriously concerned to reduce atmospheric humidity, but I have never found any need for this. Plants that need to be kept dry when resting are, of course, removed from the bench.

On all forms of capillary bench there must be direct contact between the damp surface of the bench and the compost in the pots. This means that there is no drainage material in the bottom of the pots. Modern plastic pots do not need this anyway. If clay pots are used, a small piece of glass-fibre insulating material can be inserted into the drainage hole to act as a wick. To establish capillarity, pots put on the bench are pressed firmly on to the sand with a slight twisting action. In hot weather if there is any doubt whether capillarity has been achieved, water once from above.

The compost used on all kinds of capillary bench must be well aerated if the plants are to thrive. This means that all potting is done very lightly – just a tap on the bench and a very light firming with the fingers around the edge when re-potting, but no hard ramming. The expert grower of exhibition plants may complain that this is not the way to grow a fine hardwooded plant, and he may be right. All I can say is that a mass of healthy and attractive plants can be grown with ease and success. Opinions differ as to what modifications to make to the compost for plants on capillary benches. I use John Innes composts with a little additional coarse grit or sand. I have also used soilless composts and mixtures of peat and loam-based compost. The one essential is to avoid consolidating the compost and to re-pot if a plant looks sickly for no apparent reason. It is wise to keep newly potted plants off the bench for two or three days, as those with damaged roots do not take kindly to this form of watering.

The capillary watering kits sold to amateurs are usually designed for use with capillary matting and many are only used at holiday time. Capillary matting is rather ugly and needs fairly frequent renewal, but it can be made to work well. It is essential to test the system thoroughly before a holiday as, if things go wrong, the matting dries very quickly. Various forms of float valve are used to control the water level.

For a home-made capillary bench all that is required is a level bench that is strong enough to support a couple of inches of wet sand and the pots without sagging. A solid edge to the staging is also desirable, and the whole is made waterproof with a single sheet of medium or heavy quality plastic sheeting.

The water level can be controlled in various ways. The ordinary domestic ball-cock is a rather rough instrument for making a sensitive response to very small demands for water. There are small plastic floats as used in the self-filling individual drinking bowls designed for cattle. These do not need mains-water pressure to work and the amateur plumber can fit them up. If benches are of differing heights, each level will need a separate water control consisting of one of these floats in a plastic box with a plastic tube from the water supply and another to the bottom of

A group of calceolarias (see page 40).

the bench. A tiny hole can be made in the plastic sheeting at the base of the bench and small black plastic tubing pushed gently through it, to give a waterproof joint.

Do not use transparent plastic piping as algae will grow inside it and block it in hot weather. Light coloured tanks are also a mistake. Algae will also grow on the matting. This does not matter but is ugly. The matting can be washed or treated with chemicals.

In time algae and moss will grow on the sand, and chemicals are sometimes used to prevent this. I prefer to scrape off and replace the surface of the sand occasionally and one can also wash and replace all the sand. Obtaining coarse sand in quantities of more than 7lb and less than a lorry load is the main difficulty with this system.

With capillary watering, no matter what equipment is used, one does want to be able to see at a glance whether the apparatus is working. When buying any automated equipment always ask the question: 'How do I see instantly if this system has stopped working?'

THE IRRIGATED BENCH

If it is impossible to achieve a really level surface, one can have an irrigated capillary bench. This consists of a sand-covered bench which is kept watered but is not waterproof at the edges, so that surplus water drains away. A capillary mat can also be used in this way. It is merely a way of adding to the humidity and lessening the individual watering. Capillarity is easily lost in hot weather and it does not have the reliability or usefulness of the controlled capillary bench.

POINT WATERING

There are a number of watering systems that bring water to each plant, either trickling out of adjustable nozzles or dripping from fine tubing. With these the plants may be potted in the traditional ways and the pots can stand on any freely draining staging. Trickle lines and seep-hose can also be used to water plants growing in the ground and to keep irrigated benches moist. When used on the ground a point to remember is that, although long periods of watering penetrate more deeply, a wider area of soil is dampened by more frequent watering for shorter periods.

There are a variety of drip-watering arrangements using very small-bore plastic tubing with individual tubes to each pot; these are supplied by larger-bore rigid tubing. They can have adjustable rates of drip for different plants and positions, and can be tailored to suit any pot arrangement, although an artistic arrangement of plants is made more difficult. With fine tubing the trouble to watch for is blockage of small tubes from lime in the water. These systems are often activated by turning on a tap for a time each day. To automate drip systems, high-pressure water and also electricity are desirable, but amateur kits are available using a simple syphon system. In these, water drips slowly into a small tank, which, when full, empties through the trickle or drip lines connected to it. The disadvantage of this system is that a slow drip, if left unattended for long, is apt to stop completely, while a rapid drip will give too much water.

A sophisticated system using an electric solar control, which adjusts the watering according to the weather, is available for controlling either watering or mist propagation but this is a costly solution.

Perhaps the most obvious way to water plants automatically is to imitate rain, and this is done through nozzles of a similar type to those used for mist propagation. All effective systems of this kind need a source of water at mains pressure or a special pump. In hard water districts continual spraying will leave an ugly lime deposit on both plants and greenhouse glass which is difficult to remove. Where plants needing high humidity are grown, automatic spraying may be used for damping down the floor.

Those who want to specialise in lime-hating plants in districts with very alkaline water must remember that, unless they have ample supplies of rain water, or are prepared for the considerable cost of treating the water, their plants may suffer on an automated watering system.

The more elaborate automatic watering schemes use electricity. If both water and electricity are available, there is virtually no watering problem that cannot be solved at a price. The simplest arrangement that works reliably in one's own circumstances is usually the best. One thing to bear in mind is that there is no equipment for controlling the flow of water on a small scale which it is beyond the wit of ordinary people to understand. What is happening may be boxed in or obscured by technical terms, but it is bound to be based on some fairly simple principle. This can be understood and will be explained to those determined to know. Watering arrangements once installed must remain in working order for long periods, and it is virtually impossible to keep equipment working continuously if one does not understand it. Before installing anything that might need professional servicing, it is wise to check whether this is available as well as its likely cost.

Several methods of adjusting the frequency of watering to the weather have been used with varying success. A time clock can be altered to match the season and can operate on a less than daily basis in winter, but it takes no account of whether the sun is shining or not. A solar control using a photo-electric cell has been used with success for some years. It needs to be fixed facing due south and is then activated by the amount of light falling on it. This does not necessarily match up precisely to the amount of water needed, but it is adjustable.

To turn water on and off solenoid (magnetic) valves have long been used, together with a time clock or other electronic controller. A daily watering of not less than 15 or 20 minutes can be arranged by using an ordinary time clock (as used in domestic central heating systems) together with a solenoid valve. If a very short watering time is needed, it becomes more complicated and expensive because a second time clock is necessary. The first (24 hour) time clock is set to come on for 1 hour a day and to switch on a second (1 hour) time clock which may be set for as little as 2 or 3 minutes. All this can work off mains electricity, but as it is considered safer in greenhouses to use low voltages, the electronic controllers designed for horticultural use usually have a transformer and work at 24 volts. These are linked to low-voltage solenoid valves. It is possible to have solenoids for all the various couplings of high and low voltage and water pressure, but one must be sure of what is needed. Obviously it is possible to bring the silicon chip into play and the day may soon come when the happy gardener presses a few keys by the bedside to activate all systems.

Many of us as children have watched the sluicing down of paths and the spraying of foliage in some large public or private greenhouse. Indeed the warm green smell of damp soil and the mingled scents of growing plants is what the words greenhouse and conservatory conjure up in our minds. This is the good growing atmosphere gardeners talk about. The amount of moisture in the air, and hence coolness in warm weather, is much influenced by the amount of green growth within the greenhouse or conservatory. If there is a concrete floor and a few rather dry pot plants, the temperature will rise very rapidly and the air will be far too dry.

The lavish use of hoses is hardly appropriate in the small greenhouse, but in summer there is a great need to increase the humidity in the air as well as to cool it. Some compromise needs to be made between what is desirable and what is practical. Spraying the floor morning and evening in the summer months is one way out, but the effect is not lasting in hot sunny weather and a more frequent automated spraying would be better. For orchids an electric humidifier is sometimes used if the plants warrant this

Dendrobium nobile, an epiphytic orchid suitable for the warm greenhouse.

luxury. For many plants, shade as well as humidity will be necessary, particularly if the ventilation is poor.

From October to March no extra dampness is needed, and in cool conditions the less water that is splashed about the better. In winter, hand watering should be done early in the day. The human senses are adept at judging atmospheric humidity once they know what is wanted. People tend to feel uncomfortable when the humidity falls below 50%, and this is too dry for plants. A daytime atmospheric humidity around 60 to 65% seems to be satisfactory for most plants. The humidity at night will be and should be higher.

Although mist propagation is not strictly what is meant by watering, I mention it here because it is a useful tool for those who have to be away a great deal. As well as rooting the more difficult cuttings, seeds can be raised to the pricking out stage under mist, and the plants then put on capillary benches.

In mist propagation various forms of so-called 'electronic leaf' are used to control the amount of misting. Perhaps the simplest of these is the one directly linked with the actual conditions of humidity. In this the weight of water falling as mist turns off the system, until the plastic foam sponge which has absorbed the water dries out enough to alter a weight balance and thus turns on the mist once more. The other electronic leaves depend on water connecting electrodes and then breaking the current as they dry out. These may need frequent cleaning if the water is limy. A good alternative is the solar control already described.

Soils and feeding

A simple way to start growing pot plants is to buy a bag of ready-made compost and use it straight from the bag. Today, the choice is bewildering and ever changing, as the combination of research and marketing soon establishes new composts if they prove useful in nursery practice. These are mainly for the production of young plants, which is also what many amateurs are engaged in. However, the more permanent or specimen pot plant still responds to a traditional diet and each one of us will adhere to methods found successful in our own conditions.

Until some forty years ago every keen gardener took pride in his own special mixtures of the stock ingredients and often varied the compost for each species. Then the John Innes Horticultural Institution produced a formula which gave a satisfactory soil-based compost with slight variations for seedlings and more established plants. They were called the John Innes composts, and the problem of what soil to use seemed to have been solved. These composts are still sold in great quantities and preferred by many people.

Good John Innes compost is as good as it ever was, but unfortunately it becomes rarer every day. The composts are based on a medium loam soil, which only exists in a limited area of the country and is in very short supply. Before being used for potting, turves from good pasture are supposed to be stacked for some months with an even scarcer commodity, strawy manure, and then the whole heap mixed together and screened before being sterilised. Quite apart from the labour involved, the cost of transporting such heavy materials from one part of the country to another has become uneconomic. The result is that much of the John Innes compost sold is made with unsuitable soil. It may also be difficult to find suitable loam to make up one's own compost. However, if the soil is going to be less than ideal anyway, the home-made compost may be preferable for those who have the time and inclination to prepare it.

The loam should pass through a $\frac{3}{8}$ inch (6–7mm) sieve and must be sterilised. This means bringing it up to a temperature of 200°F (93°C), and maintaining it there for twenty minutes either in a special steriliser or a saucepan over hot water.

To make John Innes seed compost, 2 parts loam, 1 part granulated peat and 1 part coarse sand (all by bulk) are mixed together, with the addition of $1\frac{1}{2}$ oz. (40g) superphosphate of lime and $\frac{3}{4}$ oz. (20g) of either finely ground chalk or limestone. These ingredients need thorough mixing.

The proportions for making John Innes potting composts are 7 parts loam, 3 parts peat and 2 parts sand. To this is added 4 oz. (115g) John Innes Base Fertilizer per bushel for the No. 1 compost, 8 oz. (225g) per bushel for No. 2, and 12 oz. (340g) for No. 3. Ground chalk or limestone is also added to the potting soils at the rate of $\frac{3}{4}$ oz. (20g) per bushel for No. 1 compost (for very young plants), $1\frac{1}{2}$ oz. (40g) for the No. 2 compost (for most plants), and 3 oz. (85g) for the No. 3 compost (which is needed for strong growing plants in large pots or tubs).

There are now some ready-made composts which are of the John Innes type but use modern slow-release fertilizers. These are sometimes in a separate sachet which enables the compost to be stored for longer without deteriorating. All loam-based composts are best used fresh. Another development is the substitution of perlite for the coarse grit or sand in the traditional mixtures. This may not be better but is certainly lighter in weight, which can be important.

A point the manufacturers seem to have overlooked is that keen gardeners like to experiment and mix their own composts. This may upset the scientist's careful formulae, but many amateurs mix ready-made soil-based and soilless composts together. A half and half mixture is popular and goes some way towards correcting the tendency of plants in peat to become top-heavy.

During the last twenty years there has been a steady increase in the use of peat-based composts. A peat and vermiculite mixture is also used, and more recently the all-peat and perlite composts have been developed. None of these have to be sterilised and they can be stored without changing their character, unlike soil.

It is an advantage of the manufactured composts, or substrates as they are sometimes called, that they are lighter in weight and more uniform than anything containing soil. Nevertheless, they are not suitable for large specimen plants and the watering technique is different from that in soil-based composts. Peat holds more water than soil but dries out more quickly, and once dry may be difficult to wet. All the same most bought pot plants are in some type of peat compost and their care is familiar to many. As the distribution of the various composts is not evenly spread over the country, amateurs need to become accustomed to one or more that are readily available locally. Pine bark and plastic waste are other materials used in some composts.

It is important to remember that plants grown in soilless composts need supplementary feeding sooner than those grown in soil-based composts, as they do not have the natural reserve of plant nutrients found in soil. The modern slow-release and chelated fertilizers are suited to peat and sand composts and have often been included in their composition.

A potting shed can be regarded either as a necessity or a luxury depending on circumstances; but obviously it is undesirable to store composts, fertilizers, pesticides or unwashed pots in the greenhouse. Where there are children, a locked cupboard for pesticides and herbicides, away from heat, frost or food, is much more important than a potting shed.

However, potting must be done and is more likely to be done successfully and at the right time if it can be done in reasonable comfort. Although there is little room to do potting in the average greenhouse, this is a bad habit that I cherish. It is warmer for both plants and people and with a portable potting bench or even a bucket of compost it is perfectly feasible. Nevertheless, a well-stocked potting shed is desirable and a well-kept one a positive pleasure.

The basic ingredients of all potting composts have been loam, sand, leafmould and well-rotted manure. Each of these is a variable substance, and it is only with experience that one comes to know the feel of a compost that is porous and open, and yet with sufficient humus to retain moisture and nutrition and to support healthy growth. Both the plants grown and the watering methods determine the most effective compost.

The choice of materials is also influenced by the beliefs of the gardener. The compost used by the growing number of people determined to use nothing but wholly organic ingredients will be different from that chosen by those who find the development of slow-release chemical fertilizers an inspiring breakthrough. The ornamental plants in our homes can live on pills and substrates and artificial light, or they can even take part in a movement back to nature whereby the wastes of men are re-cycled for plant use. I will describe both fashionable and unfashionable materials for composts.

Loam. Fibrous loam, the basis of all traditional potting mixtures, is not just garden soil but the top 4 or 5 in. (10–12.5cm) of well grazed pasture, which has been stacked for a year until the grass has rotted, leaving the fibrous soil. For making John Innes composts it is suggested that a 2 in. (5cm) layer of manure should be spread on every second layer of turves with a sprinkling of ground limestone on the alternate layers. The whole heap should be thoroughly wet right through and is then protected from heavy rain and left to rot down.

Leafmould. This vital ingredient went out of fashion and was replaced by peat; nevertheless the most dedicated gardeners have never abandoned leafmould if they have a source of supply. It is the product of the decay of leaves of deciduous trees, preferably beech and oak. If collected in autumn and turned once or twice, they break down in about eighteen months into a light fluffy substance that can be passed through a half-inch sieve. If just left lying in a wired enclosure, leaves usually take two years to decay sufficiently. It must be remembered that there will be lime in leafmould from trees on limy soil. Lime-free leafmould is a useful potting material for lime-hating and shrubby plants.

Peat. For potting composts granular sphagnum or sedge peat without too much dust or small particles is best. Peat does not contain plant food.

Sand. Sand should be coarse, clean and lime-free. Soft yellow builder's sand is not suitable for potting, nor is sea sand unless very thoroughly washed to remove salt. The sand particles should be up to $\frac{1}{8}$ inch size (3 mm).

Vermiculite. This substance is extremely light and absorbent. In a granulated form mixed with peat and fertilizers it forms one of the commercial composts. It is also available as a sterile medium without nutrients. Cuttings can be rooted in it or in a mixture of peat and vermiculite. It is so light that young plants can be lifted from it without damaging the finest roots.

Perlite. This is also a light and absorbent substance created by the heat treatment of volcanic rock. It can be used in a similar manner to vermiculite and is also used in orchid composts, sometimes being substituted for the grit or sand in John Innes type composts. It is available in a variety of granule sizes for different purposes.

Garden compost. The compost heap of decayed vegetable matter is a valuable source of humus with a nutrient value that will vary according to how well it is made. For potting it needs to be very well made, if it is not to be full of weed seeds and harmful organisms.

A compost heap should have a well aerated base of coarse material such as twigs. On this 6 in. layers (15cm) of vegetable matter (excluding woody stalks and seeding weeds) are interspersed with 2 in. layers (5cm) of animal manure, if possible, or a good sprinkling of any organic manures of animal origin, such as dried blood, fish manure or hoof and horn. Following this comes a sprinkling of earth mixed with wood ashes and lime, or lime alone. These three layers are repeated until the heap is completed. To heat up properly, it needs to be about 6ft by 4ft (1.8 × 1.2 m) in area and not more than 5 or 6 ft high (1.5 or 1.8m). For small heaps a compost box or bin is helpful. Lawn mowings and fallen leaves, which tend to matt together into a slimy mass, should only be added in thin layers or mixed with other refuse. Comfrey plants are sometimes grown to provide extra green material to rot down. If animal manures are lacking, there are both natural and chemical activators which can be added to hasten decomposition. The whole heap needs to be moist but not sodden, and a ventilation hole made with a crowbar in the centre is a good idea. The compost should reach a high temperature during decomposition and be reduced to a dark brown sweet-smelling earth. If it dries out or cools down at an early stage, this will not be achieved.

Wood ashes. These should be kept dry until used. They are an organic source of potash and are sometimes added to composts, particularly if the soil is heavy.

Lime. Lime is not a fertilizer in the usual sense, although it supplies calcium which many plants need. It improves the texture of clay soils and corrects acidity, but it should not be applied to soil with a pH of 6.5 or above (pH is a measure of acidity). The neutral point is pH 7.0. Above is alkaline and below acid. A pH of 6.3 is considered best for John Innes compost and pH 5.3 to 5.5 for peat and sand composts. For lime-hating plants the pH needs to be below 6.0. One can discover the pH of the soil with a simple soil testing outfit. One can also ignore the whole thing and hope it is all right!

Manure. Cow manure is perhaps the most generally satisfactory for horticultural purposes, if obtainable, but horse manure is good for heating up a slow compost heap. Poultry manure is chemically rich unless it has been spoilt by exposure to the weather. It should be stored dry under cover. No manure should be used in a greenhouse border until it is in a well-rotted state, but fresh manure may be added to the compost heap.

Fish meal. This is an organic source of nitrogen, phosphorus and potash and is a useful fertilizer for the greenhouse border.

Bonemeal. This slow-acting fertilizer, containing phosphorus and a little nitrogen, suffered an eclipse owing to the fear of its transmitting disease, but is now always heat treated.

Poinsettias (*Euphorbia pulcherrima*) are popular plants at Christmas time (see page 56).

When plants are growing strongly and the pots are full of roots, the question of additional feeding arises. Some understanding of the processes of plant growth is helpful. We all realise that air, water, light and sufficient warmth must be supplied for growth to take place. Then the leaves will be able to manufacture sugars, starches and proteins, while the roots obtain the various essential minerals and moisture from the soil. Nitrogen, phosphates and potassium, sometimes cryptically referred to as NPK, are the most used and most likely to need replacement. They are present in various proportions in all the compound fertilizers and liquid feeds. Those designed for foliage plants will have more nitrogen, whereas those intended for quick growing flowering plants will have more phosphates and those for tomatoes more potassium. A tomato fertilizer is a convenient source of potash for the occasional feeding of most plants. A frequent error of amateurs is to confine themselves to one liquid feed meant for foliage house plants and then to be amazed when flowering is disappointing.

The precise and detailed needs of many plants are not known, and until recently the essential trace elements found in natural soils could not be included in fertilizers or composts. Now the dedicated gardener can use slow-release fertilizers and many trace elements fused into microscopic glass pellets, and these are even to be found in some commercial composts. Another possibility is the foliar feed whereby plants absorb nutrients through their leaves when sprayed with the diluted feed. This is a quick pick-me-up when things have gone wrong.

The secret of feeding is to give little and often and never more than is suggested on the packet. Plants that are resting do not need feeding. The re-potting of a sickly or seriously pot-bound plant will do far more good than feeding, and, if the roots are decayed or being attacked by some pest, feeding will not help.

Plants from seed

Sowing tiny seeds and watching the whole process develop, no matter how long it takes, is a never-ending pleasure to those who become deeply involved in gardening. At the same time there is nothing more maddening than careful sowing, a long wait, and then no results. Many of us will never attempt to acquire the right mental attitude to raise rare shrubs or difficult alpines from seed. But there is room for all tastes in the greenhouse and a wide variety of reliable seeds will give rapid and predictable results with reasonable care and reasonable luck. Some plants regarded as difficult are in fact easy, if one can sow fresher seed than is often available in a packet. The length of time seed remains viable is extremely varied and greatly affected by the way it is kept. Although one is advised not to discard pans of rare seeds for two or three years, this is unpractical and depressing in the conditions of the average small greenhouse.

The equipment used for seed sowing under glass ranges from the fast disappearing clay seed pan and wooden box through plastic trays, pots and pans to peat pots and compressed soil blocks as well as the plastic cast-offs of modern living. Every amateur evolves a personal method, but all successful arrangements ensure a temperature sufficient to allow germination and moisture that is constant without being excessive. It is sometimes said that the ideal temperature for germination of seeds is 10°F above the optimum growing temperature of the plant concerned. This is only a very rough guide and one cannot give each packet of seed a different temperature. As 21°C (70°F) is satisfactory for the germination of a great many seeds of greenhouse and bedding plants, most seed raisers are designed to raise the temperature to this level. The simpler types lift the temperature but do not have thermostatic control, so that one must guard against the sun shining on them. The most elaborate kinds with both soil and air heating on separate thermostats are very costly. However, soil warming cables can be put into benches or frames and there are many ways of arranging a warm corner in a cooler greenhouse. The highest temperature is only required until the seeds germinate. All seeds need to be sown much more thinly than comes naturally, with the smallest ones merely pressed lightly into the surface and the larger ones buried to their own depth in the compost.

The traditional way of covering seed boxes is a sheet of glass and a sheet of brown paper or newspaper. The glass should be turned each day to remove condensation and let in fresh air. Many seed-raisers have stiff plastic covers and only need shading from sunlight. No matter how the seeds are covered, daily inspection is advisable since they must have good light as soon as they germinate. A few plants, including *Primula obconica* and *P. sinensis*, germinate best in light and some only in the dark.

A realistic assessment of how many seedlings can be grown to maturity may mean that only quite small receptacles are needed. I use ½ in. (12mm) square pots, which fit closely together in a seed tray. This goes into a simple seed raiser in my kitchen. The moment any seedlings appear, they are moved to stronger light and cooler conditions. They must never dry out or be allowed to stop growing; therefore early pricking out is usually advised. This is always a matter of judgement if the weather is bad and the temperature rather low, but crowding does weaken growth.

Most plants are pricked out into larger, deeper trays about 2 inches (5cm) apart in a slightly richer compost. These are easier to keep evenly moist by hand watering than individual small pots. However, if one does not want enough plants to fill the boxes, individual plastic pots may be better, particularly on capillary benches. Quantities of seedlings urgently needing pricking out at the same moment are one of the nightmares of gardening.

Here are some suggestions for plants to grow from seed for greenhouse decoration with sowing dates and the approximate time taken to flower. Annuals are marked A, biennials B, perennials P. MWT is the minimum winter temperature advised for over-wintering.

Abutilon × hybridum. P. Spring, about 16 weeks. MWT 7°C (45°F).
Alonsoa. P, grown as A. March to May. About 16 weeks.
Asparagus meyerii. P. Spring. Foliage plant. MWT 7°C (45°F).
Begonia (fibrous rooted). P. February or March. Nearly 6 months.
Brachycome (Swan river daisy). A. March. About 12 weeks.
Browallia. P. March or June. About 6 months. MWT 10°C (50°F) for winter flowers.
Calceolaria. A and P. June for flowering following spring. MWT 7°C (45°F).
Campanula fragilis and *C. isophylla.* P. Trailing. Spring. About 16 weeks. MWT 4°C (40°F).
Celosia. B. March to flower in about 20 weeks. Larger plants from autumn sowing. MWT 4°C (40°F).

Cineraria. B. May to July for flowering November to March. MWT 7°C (45°F).

Coleus. P as A. Early spring in heat. Foliage plant. Discard autumn.

Cuphea. A and P. March about 16 weeks. MWT 7°C (45°F).

Cyclamen. P. June to August. 15 or 16 months. MWT 7°C (45°F).

Didiscus. A. Spring. About 18 weeks.

Eccremocarpus. P. climber. Early spring for flower same year. MWT 4°C (40°F).

Eucnide. A. March or April. About 15 weeks.

Exacum. B. March to June for flowering August to December. MWT at least 10°C (50°F).

Freesia. P. April to June. About 7 months. MWT 7°C (45°F).

Gerbera. P. March or when new seed available. About 15 months for tall kinds but new compact hybrids flower same year. MWT 10°C (50°F) for reliable winter flowering.

Gilia rubra. B. Early spring for late summer and autumn or July to over-winter and flower next year. MWT 7°C (45°F).

Grevillea robusta. P. March. Foliage plant. MWT 7°C (45°F).

Heliotropium (Cherry pie) P. March. About 15 weeks.

Hypoestes sanguinolenta. P. Foliage and house plant. MWT 16°C (60°F).

Impatiens. A. and P, grown as A. Spring in warmth. About 11 weeks. MWT 10°C (50°F) to over-winter.

Limonium suworowii. A. Early spring for summer flowering.

Lobelia tenuior. A. Spring for summer and summer for winter in cool greenhouse.

Nemesia. A. March to June. About 13 weeks.

Nierembergia caerulea. P. March and April for late summer. Frost-free to over-winter.

Pelargonium (Geranium) P. The hybrids sown in heat from January flower in 4 to 5 months according to temperature. MWT 7°C (45°F).

Petunia. P, grown as A. April. About 14 weeks.

Plumbago capensis. P. climber. Spring. 18 months. MWT 4°C (40°F).

Primula acaulis (modern hybrids) and *P. auricula.* March to May. For winter and spring in unheated and frost-free greenhouse.

Primula × kewensis and *P. malacoides.* May to June for winter. MWT 4°C (40°F).

Primula obconica and *P. sinensis.* May to June for winter. MWT 4°C (40°F).

Punica granatum 'Nana' (dwarf pomegranate). Spring for autumn. Frost-free.

Rehmannia. P. May for following year. Frost-free.

Opposite above: Primulas provide colour in winter; this is a form of
Primula obconica (p. 41).
Opposite below: Cinerarias can be grown from seed to flower in the
winter (p. 41).
Top left: Pelargoniums are popular and easy to grow from seed or
cuttings (pp. 41, 48).
Top right: *Coleus* are grown for their decorative foliage (see page 51).
Above left: *Campanula isophylla*, a pretty little trailing plant (see
page 40).
Above right: The well known Busy Lizzie (*Impatiens*) easily grown from
seeds or cuttings (see page 41).

Rosa. P. Fairy rose. March to flower in 10 weeks.

Salpiglossis. A. March and April about 20 weeks. August for May in slight heat.

Schizanthus. A. August for March and April, spring for late summer. Frost-free.

Streptocarpus. P. January or February in warmth for autumn or up to July for following summer. MWT 10°C (50°F).

Thunbergia. A. Late March. About 15 weeks.

Torenia. A. March and April. About 15 weeks.

Trachelium. P. Early spring. About 23 weeks or June for next year. MWT 7°C (45°F).

Schizanthus hybrids are available in a wide range of colours.

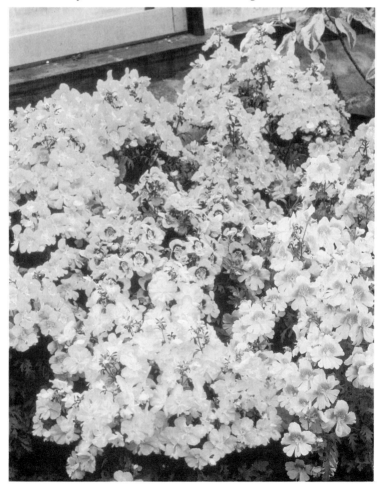

Plants from cuttings

The greenhouse favourites grown from cuttings are in themselves enough to keep every greenhouse full of bloom all the year round, as well as providing a special hobby for a wide variety of people. The actual process of taking cuttings has been revolutionised in recent years for the less skilled. Hormone rooting powders hasten rooting and make difficult species easier to strike, while the plastic bag has created a simple way of ensuring a moist environment for a potful of cuttings until rooting takes place. Mist propagation is a sophisticated option, but it is a luxury for those who do not need to raise many plants.

Although there will always be room for judgement and experience in the choice and timing of difficult cuttings, the miracle of reproducing an exact replica of an admired plant at will from a small piece is open to all.

In general terms it is the vigorous young shoot, which has not yet reached the point of flowering or ripened its wood, that roots most readily. There are green tip cuttings, semi-ripe cuttings and hardwood cuttings, as well as leaf and root cuttings, but the favourite greenhouse plants in this chapter are increased by young shoots. These need to be neatly severed, with a sharp knife or razor blade, just beneath the node or joint and put into their rooting medium while still crisp and fresh.

The compost for cuttings should hold moisture yet drain freely, and there are many alternatives. The John Innes formula is 1 part loam, 2 parts granulated peat and 3 parts coarse sand, all measured in bulk. Peat and sand in equal proportions is a much favoured mixture, while peat and sand, vermiculite or perlite are often used. Under mist pure sand is satisfactory, and it can be used without mist so long as it never dries. For cuttings that are not going to be potted up separately as soon as they have rooted, equal parts of loam, peat and sand provide more nutriment; and equal quantities of John Innes potting compost and sand is yet another alternative.

In any case the moisture of air and soil round the cuttings must never fail before they are rooted. Then they are gradually exposed to the air, first by opening and subsequently by removing the plastic bag or other covering.

In order to create enough plants for a group of ground cover in the garden, and for replacement of tender shrubs liable to be killed in a hard winter, some propagation is essential. Also, kind friends offer cuttings, for which unexpected gift the keen gardener is always ready with a plastic bag to take them home without wilting.

A majority of greenhouse plants are propagated from cuttings, and there are four favourites which for many are the principal purpose and pleasure of a greenhouse.

Perpetual flowering carnations are irresistible to some and merely a curiosity to others. The necessity here is to have healthy virus-free plants and not to keep them for more than two years. There are specialist nurserymen raising virus-free stock; they will often give advice to the beginner. Little heat is needed, but plenty of air and good winter light are essential. There needs to be room for the plants to grow tall, and red spider must be effectively controlled. A minimum winter temperature of 7°C (45°F) is desirable, as winter is the principal flowering season and cut flowers the main purpose. Cuttings can be rooted from November to March, and spring is the time to buy rooted cuttings to start a collection.

Chrysanthemums are the favourite flower of countless enthusiasts in temperate climates, as well as a major horticultural and artistic preoccupation in Japan. There is a good basis for such universal acclaim, for not only is there a great variety of flower size and type from which to choose but a spectacular response to skilled cultivation and training. Chrysanthemums also brighten the dark days of our autumn and early winter and provide exotic forms for flower arrangement.

Clearing out the greenhouse completely in summer and replacing the large plants with fresh young cuttings full of promise each spring are two aspects of chrysanthemum growing that appeal to many. Cuttings root at 7°C (45°C) and high temperatures are never needed. Healthy stock is important here too.

The fuchsia is no less adaptable in the variety of ways in which it can be trained and grown and also responds to skill in cultivation. The flowering season of fuchsias can be increased by the manipulation of daylength, as is done with chrysanthemums. As they naturally have a very long flowering season and cuttings strike easily at almost any time of year, there is no need for the amateur to fuss with extra lighting. Longer days induce flower buds to form, whereas the chrysanthemum is a short-day plant that has to be blacked out in the summer to initiate flowering.

Where there is little heat or space, fuchsias can be overwintered by allowing them to become dormant in autumn, when watering is gradually reduced so that leaves fall and the wood ripens. They can take three to four months complete rest, but the root ball should be neither frozen nor dust dry during this time.

Above: Chrysanthemums brighten the greenhouse during autumn and winter and also provide cut flowers for the house.
Below: A well-stocked greenhouse with a mass of colour provided by fuchsias, coleus and lobelias.

They are then cut back and started into growth in February or March. Autumn cuttings, or young plants being grown as standards, have to be kept growing through the winter, for which at least 7°C (45°F) is needed and 10°C (50°F) preferred.

Again skill in cultivation brings great rewards. A poorly grown fuchsia is a poor thing indeed. A neutral or lime-free soil, and plenty of judicious feeding, and well-timed training are essential for real success. The plants are attractive to white fly but otherwise reasonably healthy. A constant stream of new cultivars, as well as the very large selection of established varieties, means that there is an overwhelming choice.

Perhaps the most universal favourite of the unskilled as well as the specialist is the geranium, more properly called the zonal pelargonium. Since its first fashionable success in Victorian times, the pelargoniums have been greatly developed and also new species discovered.

Today there is something for everyone and a flow of new cultivars from the United States and Australia as well as Europe. The regal or show pelargoniums, flowering mainly from April to June, can be huge bushy plants with magnificent velvety flowers for the decoration of spacious places. Fortunately even more floriferous and adaptable dwarf regals have been created and there are a few miniatures. But all can be grown to a modest size, if confined to fairly small pots and renewed yearly from cuttings.

'The Czar', a zonal pelargonium grown for its striking foliage and delicate flowers.

Zonal pelargoniums have been produced in such enormous numbers and brilliant colours for summer bedding, that not everyone realises the scope of the many kinds which, though they would not make a show in the open in one of our wet summers, are nevertheless good greenhouse and conservatory plants. A visit to a geranium nursery can be a revelation. There are even specialists in the miniature forms, and no greenhouse is too small to have a fascinating collection.

In recent years bedding geraniums that are raised from seed each year have been so much improved that they are often preferred for municipal bedding. These are usually raised in heat very early in the year and treated with hormone dwarfing agents to encourage early flowers and a better shape. The seed is costly and should have a temperature of 18°C (65°F) to germinate. They take much more water than the old geraniums and will not flower before July if conditions are poor. They respond well to automatic watering. All members of this family are very easily increased by cuttings, which need 7°C (45°F) to over-winter happily but survive much abuse.

As with so many plants constantly renewed from cuttings, there is much virus-infected stock, which is why seed-raised plants have become popular, otherwise they are healthy and long-suffering given sufficient ventilation and freedom from frost. The danger of spreading virus infection has led the professionals to dispense with the knife when taking cuttings, but amateurs can use discarded razor blades or sterilise the knife between each cutting if there are only a few. Zonal pelargoniums are among the few cuttings best left uncovered for rooting, but as with all cuttings there must be shade from direct sunshine.

To produce a shapely pot plant with plenty of flowering shoots usually requires encouraging the early development of side shoots, and sometimes the prevention of flowering before maturity for the best results.

"Nip out the growing point at 6 inches high" is a frequent instruction in horticulture and could be applied to any of the plants I have mentioned. However, so much thought has been given to the accurate timing of chrysanthemum blooms for show and to disbudding to increase their size, that any serious grower will follow a much more elaborate regime than I could detail here.

The training of woody pot plants is an art that has largely been lost in the last hundred years and can be learnt only by practice and example. In a small greenhouse or conservatory there would be room only for one or two elaborately trained specimen plants, and the emphasis must be on young plants and those that are naturally compact in growth.

Foliage plants

In the confined space of the small greenhouse all foliage is important. Even flowering plants with large coarse leaves are unlikely to be worth growing. No one should ignore foliage plants, for they are attractive all the year while many flowers only last a short time. They are helpful, too, in avoiding the flat effect of many small pot plants grown on one level, for there are trailers, trees, and palms, as well as the ferns and other shade lovers that grow happily under the staging. Flower arrangers will want trails of foliage to pick, while the strange forms of succulents are also effective in a mixed display. Some coloured leaves are as brilliant as any blossoms, and the cool greys and greens separate and enhance the brighter colours. In a conservatory one is particularly likely to want permanent plants in larger pots.

In the north facing or otherwise shaded greenhouse, plants grown for their foliage will be the mainstay. It must be remembered that ferns need a damp atmosphere as well as shade. This is difficult to maintain in a small greenhouse or conservatory in summer even with artificial shading, if the structure is in a hot position.

The foliage plants now grown as house plants enjoy warmth, but the glass will probably need shading from April to October. Most of them need a minimum winter temperature of at least 10°C (50°F) to do more than endure the winter, but all can be propagated and re-potted and generally encouraged to grow better, if there is a greenhouse available in the warmer months. The highly ornamental rex begonias and palms also appreciate shaded warmth in summer. Although there may not be room for palms to grow large, they develop slowly and most will survive in the cool greenhouse or conservatory if gradually accustomed to cooler conditions.

Almost everyone seems to have a soft spot for grey leaves, which nature has endowed with a protective tomentum or silvery hairs to protect them from powerful sunlight or wind dessication. Many such plants are valued in the garden but often lost in our wet winters, so that small plants over-wintered in the greenhouse may serve the double purpose of preserving the stock and providing a useful foil for the brighter colours.

The grey-leaved plants do not want warmth, only freedom from frost and not too rich a soil. The better forms of *Senecio cineraria* and *Centaurea gymnocarpa* are well worth preserving and cuttings can be rooted at the end of the summer. *Helichrysum petiolatum* is another silver plant that can be decorative in a cold greenhouse. *Pyrethrum ptarmacaefolium* with silver leaves of a lacey fineness is also raised from seed or cuttings. It is at its best in its second year if pruned in March.

Pelargoniums provide a number of coloured leaved and variegated plants. *Pelargonium graveolens* 'Lady Plymouth' with finely divided grey and white leaves is a favourite of mine. The cypress-like *P. crispum variegatum* with small crinkled cream and green foliage and the well-named ivy leaf pelargonium 'L'Elegante' that is green and white, and pink as well, if kept on the dry side, are other suggestions.

Amongst succulents, kalanchoes also provide a choice, *K. marmorata* has blue-grey leaves with brown freckles, while those of the plushy *K. tomentosa* are brown tipped. *Kalanchoe pumila* is a small grey-leaved plant for the front of the staging or a hanging basket. It has pink flowers in spring. These all thrive in 7°C (45°F) and are very easily renewed from cuttings.

Asparagus fern is well known and there are several forms. *Asparagus meyerii* with elegant plumes of foliage is an unusual plant to raise from seed and so is the pink spotted *Hypoestes sanguinolenta*, sometimes called the polka dot plant.

For coloured leaves everyone knows *Coleus*, which can be rapidly grown from cuttings to make plants of any size according to the warmth and skill lavished on them. Many brilliant kinds can also be raised from seed. In the warm greenhouse or conservatory codiaeums are no less colourful all the year round. Indeed in warmth the choice becomes very large with creepers and climbers, coloured veining and rich velvety surfaces.

The polka dot plant, *Hypoestes sanguinolenta* (see also p. 41).

Bulbs, corms and tubers

Everyone loves bulbous plants in winter and early spring, and few of us fail to be impressed by the showy tuberous begonias or the cyclamen, hippeastrums and gloxinias in their season. Even the less widely grown but no less handsome *Haemanthus*, *Lachenalia*, *Nerine* and *Vallota* rouse the greatest enthusiasm when seen in flower. It is the dormant period of the bulbous plant that is its undoing. A bulb, tuber, corm or rhizome is a storage vessel, where the essentials for next year's flowering are kept safely until the favourable season for growth comes round again. Many of the most exotic bulbs from the southern hemisphere adapt fairly readily to a dry period of rest during our winters, instead of enduring a summer drought at home. However, under glass it is up to us to signal the changing seasons and this is where we often fail. It takes some foresight and an organised approach to grow the more tender bulbs successfully year after year, which is the way that brings real satisfaction.

Although generally speaking the spring flowering bulbs are planted or re-potted in autumn and the summer flowering ones are planted in spring, some fleshy rooted plants are never wholly dormant and others have a very brief rest, which does not fit in with the commercial arrangements for dry bulbs. For those who become interested in the more unusual bulbous plants, there is plenty to learn, quite apart from the possible thrills of travelling to see such plants in their native habitat. The serious collector of rare bulbs often has a bulb frame. This is a raised bed of freely draining soil, which can be protected from the rain or cold at the appropriate seasons for summer ripening or winter dormancy. Here the bulbs can be grouped according to seasonal behaviour and allowed to grow naturally. This method does not create a show of bloom at any one time, but it does allow the best development of the smaller rarer bulbs, the habits of which are sometimes little known. Every bulb has its preferred position in the soil and most will adjust themselves to their natural depth in time, no matter how they are planted. This can be startling, as those who have raised bulbs from seed will know. After sowing seeds in a pot, one may find small bulbs in the gravel or capillary bench beneath it.

Although the idea of raising bulbous plants from seed is usually rejected by the beginner, it is not necessarily a slow process. The

Iris reticulata 'Cantab', a small hardy bulb suitable for the unheated greenhouse (see p. 54).

beautiful *Lilium philippinense* can be flowered in nine months; freesias flower in seven months from a spring sowing and are very easy to grow. The fifteen or sixteen months it can take to raise a hybrid cyclamen from seed is more exacting, but some of the smaller newer hybrids are very much quicker.

The problem of how to rest a cyclamen corm always provokes conflicting advice, which only goes to show how adaptable fleshy rooted plants are to any steady regime. The secret is to keep them dry but not totally dry, from when the leaves start yellowing until that awkward moment when everyone is on holiday in August and the cyclamen is ready to be re-potted. Do not worry; leave it in the shade outside the back door where the rain will reach it, and you will be reminded to re-pot it on your return.

The small hardy wild cyclamen species, sometimes grown in pans in the unheated greenhouse, can be difficult to start into growth when bought dry and may remain dormant for a year, which is disconcerting.

Begonias have tiny seeds and need warmth from the time they are sown in January, and so it is much less demanding to grow them from tubers in spring. The same is true of gloxinias. If they are to be enjoyed again the following year, they must be dried off gradually in October, so that the fleshy roots ripen and the foliage dries off completely before they are stored. They can remain in their pots or be put in dry peat and kept frost free, preferably at a temperature around 10°C (50°F). They are started into growth again in March. The fascinating Rechsteineria leucotricha is a less well-known plant that is easily raised from seed in spring and may have a small flower in its first season. It has a corm that grows larger each year and needs only a fairly brief dry rest in midwinter in the cool greenhouse.

In an unheated greenhouse only the hardy bulbs can be grown in winter, but they will flower several weeks earlier than those in the open. Amongst the smaller hardy bulbs that are attractive in pots in January are the early crocus species and Iris histrioides 'Major', followed by the yellow I. danfordiae and the scented I. reticulata. One of my favourites is the scarlet multi-flowered Tulipa praestans, but there are plenty to choose from besides the obvious hyacinths and daffodils.

The Vallota is an evergreen bulbous plant that is shy-flowering until pot-bound and may be difficult to start if sold as a dry bulb. The big scarlet flowers in late summer are worth having. Another evergreen with fleshy roots is Clivia and this too can remain in the same pot for years. Its handsome orange or yellow flowers usually appear in late spring.

Perhaps the most spectacular of all glasshouse bulbs are the Hippeastrum hybrids (often wrongly called Amaryllis) that produce the largest flowers in scarlet, white, pink or orange, to silence the most querulous visitor. They often manage two spikes of four flowers each, although they occasionally miss a year and lose friends that way. Early spring is the planting time, except for those specially prepared for Christmas flowering, which will join the others in blooming in April and May in subsequent years. They need to be gradually induced to rest in September, until they show signs of life in spring. Some obstinately remain evergreen and all need 10°C (50°F) in winter.

Other fleshy rooted flowering plants to try in the warmer greenhouse or conservatory are Achimenes, Gesneria, Gloriosa, Haemanthus and Smithiantha. Suggestions for cooler conditions would include the winter flowering Lachenalia, hybrid nerines flowering in autumn and the handsome Veltheimia, which are ornamental through the winter and flower in spring. In an unheated or just frost-free greenhouse, the nearly hardy bulbous plants sometimes grown outdoors are worth considering. These include Agapanthus, Ixia, Nerine bowdenii, Sparaxis, Streptanthera and Tigridia (see p. 7).

Climbers and shrubs

There is no distinct division between climbers and trailers under glass, or indeed between climbers and shrubs if the latter can be persuaded to cover a wall. In a conservatory climbers give a furnished look and may also be used to give shade. The passion flower (*Passiflora caerulea*) is particularly useful for this (see p. 2). All climbers and shrubs planted in the ground under glass will have to endure frequent and severe pruning, if they are not to overwhelm the place quite soon. Nevertheless, it is a mistake not to grow any climbers and hard-wooded plants.

In a small structure space is so important that one must either confine the roots in a pot or tub or limit oneself to one climber trained up to the roof or back wall. All the favourite conservatory plants are inclined to be rampant. The passion flower can be confined to a tub for a time and pruned hard back in winter. The same is true of the sweet-scented *Jasminum polyanthum* that will root at every joint and grow twelve foot in a season, although young plants blooming in a 5-inch pot look innocent enough. The pale blue *Plumbago capensis* is by nature a big sprawling shrub with a long flowering season. It is quick and easy from seed or cuttings, takes hard pruning and will even submit to a pot, but cannot really do itself justice that way.

The Australian blue bell creeper (*Sollya heterophylla*) also has pale blue flowers and grows quickly from seed, but is of modest proportions. The beautiful *Lapageria rosea*, the national flower of Chile, must have a lime-free soil. It is evergreen with small neat leaves, and is slow-growing when confined to a pot. It likes shady cool conditions and the rosy pendant flowers are striking. (See p. 6).

There is much to be said for a modest climber that dies back and makes a fresh growth from the root each year. Nature has limited its scope and you do not have to harden your heart and chop it down. *Gloriosa superba* and particularly *G. rothschildiana* is always greatly admired and may reach 6 ft (1.8m), but is a dry root for half the year.

Tropaeolum tricolor from Chile is a tuberous rooted climber of moderate vigour that dies down in mid-summer and rests until growth starts again. Light support will be needed for the twining growths wreathed with scarlet and black flowers in spring.

Fuchsias have been mentioned in other chapters and can be

trained to any shape, but *F. procumbens* from New Zealand is a curious trailing plant for pots that few would recognise as a fuchsia. The yellow and purple flowers are followed by red berries.

Those with a wall to cover in a sunny conservatory may be attracted by bougainvilleas. If happy, they ramp with thorny branches, but if unhappy they may forget to flower and be covered with greenfly. Plants as diverse as *Begonia fuchsioides* and zonal pelargoniums can be trained against a wall, and the important thing is to choose a plant that is not too attractive to pests. One of these, the orange flowered *Streptosolen jamesonii*, is an amenable bush for training upwards, and its hanging flowers look their best from below.

A group of climbers that are not too thrusting in a small space are the hoyas. Their clustered blossoms look more like wax or icing sugar than any form of plant life. *Hoya bella* is a tricky but beautiful basket plant for the warm greenhouse and *H. carnosa* a less demanding climber in a pot in cool conditions.

Small shrubs in pots often arrive as gifts, such as the Christmas azaleas, and it becomes a matter of pride to keep them from year to year. Plunged outdoors in light shade from June to October and re-potted if necessary in April, they can be kept going for years by those who manage never to forget to water them. They should have 7°C (45°F) and a moist atmosphere to bring on the bloom.

The modern poinsettia (*Euphorbia pulcherrima*) is less demanding than its forebears, but prefers a temperature of 13°C (55°F) and regular watering. After a nearly dry and slightly cooler rest in late winter it can be kept for another year, if repotted in April and kept warm and damp. It will flower later and be much larger, as it is grown commercially with chemical dwarfing and controlled day length(see p. 38).

Hibiscus rosa-sinensis is now a popular house plant that flowers for months but needs 13°C (55°F) in winter.

Camellias are irresistible in flower and valuable in a north facing cool or cold conservatory. They are best outside in summer as they are hardy plants only needing protection for their winter flowers.

For spring the mimosa best suited in size and slowness of growth to a confined space is *Acacia armata*, with narrow stems of small leaves dotted with little mimosa puffs. Perhaps the dwarf pomegranate *Punica granatum* 'Nana' quickly grown from seed to flower at 3 inches tall (7.5cm) is the nearest thing to a mini shrub designed for the beginner in a mini greenhouse.

Specialisation

In earlier chapters I have mentioned some of the favourite flowering plants that often capture the whole attention of amateurs. Perpetual flowering carnations, chrysanthemums, fuchsias and the various pelargoniums are all attractive plants with long flowering seasons that respond well to skilled cultivation. Each one of them can become an absorbing hobby. Many people find it more satisfying to know a great deal about a limited subject than to have a smattering of knowledge over a wide field.

One way of specialising is in groups of related plants. The gesneriads are an interesting family that have become more freely available in recent years. The saintpaulia or African violet started the craze, as it is so widely grown as a house plant. It needs a warm greenhouse to be happy, as do *Columnea*, *Episcea*, *Hypocyrta* and *Smithiantha*. *Streptocarpus* has free flowering and relatively tolerant hybrids seen both in the cool greenhouse and on the window sill and there are also strange and interesting species. Some gesneriads have underground storage organs that are dormant in winter and can be grown in any greenhouse in summer. *Achimenes*, gloxinia (*Sinningia*), *Kohleria* and *Rechsteineria* are the best known.

Most people either love or hate the cactus family, but enough are interested to support a very active national society and countless local groups. Today there is no need or excuse for growing plants imported from native habitats, many of which have been devastated by commercial exploitation. Specialist growers in Britain and elsewhere can supply an infinite variety of nursery-grown plants, while enthusiasts also exchange seed and plants amongst themselves.

Those who decide to specialise in cacti, rare succulents, or the wild species of orchids should be particularly vigilant about the sources of their plants and the need not to decimate their original habitat. Although the individual can do little to safeguard a threatened species, every person who unthinkingly buys plants collected in the wild is encouraging this destructive trade.

Orchids are a specialisation that should be considered before the greenhouse is built, as one can greatly improve the chances of success by a suitable choice of structure. Adequate ridge ventilation, box ventilators low down and specially designed staging to aid humidity are also helpful, while a high degree of atmospheric humidity and proper shading are essential. Orchids are very long-lived and extremely interesting plants worthy of study. I believe their greater appeal to men than to women is partly because men are less concerned with the general decorative effect in a green-house and more intrigued by the strange, the rare and the scented.

Orchids are particular rather than delicate. They will survive poor handling, but fail to flower unless the nature of their invididual seasonal growth is understood. This cannot happen without experience. Orchids are not an expensive hobby if one has the patience to wait for young plants to reach the flowering stage. It is, however, necessary to have a minimum winter temperature of at least 10°C (50°F) to start a collection, and 13°C (55°F) is needed for many of the more interesting orchids. Although the traditional orchid composts, based on osmunda fibre, have almost disappeared owing to their cost today, there are simpler modern counterparts that make potting very much easier. Many orchids are epiphytic (see p. 32) and cling to trees and rocks in nature, which is the main reason why special composts are necessary. Nurserymen selling orchids recognize the need for starting off beginners on the right lines, and they usually both sell and explain the use of the various materials needed.

Bromeliads are another group of epiphytic plants enjoying similar conditions to orchids but they are much less demanding. Some are sold as house plants and enjoy warmth and shade, while others endure much cooler and drier conditions than orchids. Many can be grown without soil fixed to artificial trees or other objects, and regularly sprayed with water and weak feeds. They have a wide variety of strange and long-lasting flowers.

I believe that everyone specialising in one plant or one group of plants needs either to join a specialist society or to find at least one friend or neighbour with the same interest. Quite apart from the fact that new friends are often made through a shared interest, seeds, plants and cuttings are exchanged, together with much practical knowledge that cannot easily be found in books. One needs, too, the inspiration of seeing other collections.

Pests

No matter what views one may hold about pests and diseases or poison sprays, the golden rule under glass is to start clean. With the new greenhouse there is no problem, but in the year-round warmth of heated greenhouses there is bound to be a gradual build up of unwanted guests unless preventive steps are taken. Some may be engaged in eating others and there is much talk of preserving beneficial predators and parasites.

We want to prevent pests or diseases from consuming or disfiguring our plants and to do so without endangering ourselves or our children. This is not as simple as it sounds, because some of the most damaging insects gradually become resistant to remedies that are regularly applied. Varying the chemicals used prevents a build-up of pest resistance.

Our first thought must always be to avoid introducing pests or diseases into the greenhouse. It is worth being quite ruthless about this. Every plant needs the most careful examination before being added to a collection. The soft growing points and the undersides of the leaves are the places to look. This may sound fussy, but two weeks isolation followed by another close examination is even more effective. If in doubt spray with pesticide.

Some pests will always be with us, unless we are willing to have a continuous discharge of some chemical or a frequent and regular spraying or fumigation in the greenhouse. I would rather keep a sharp look out and spray the enemies when seen.

There are four extremely persistent greenhouse pests that one needs to keep under control, and recognition of these is essential. These are mealybugs, red spider mites, whitefly and aphids. Among the lesser evils to look out for are ants, earwigs, scales and thrips.

Mealybugs. These creatures which look like tiny white woodlice are clearly visible to those with normal sight, and their presence is usually first noticed as a small patch of white wool,which means they are breeding. Fortunately they do not spread rapidly in the early stages, but they are hard to kill. Picking off each insect with a pin or painting them and their eggs with methylated spirits are two effective methods for small infestation. This pest is the only major pest of cacti and succulents and can spread to woody plants if allowed to do so.

In heavier infestations, nicotine, malathion or one of the newer systemic insecticides, such as dimethoate, may be used either as sprays or, in the case of the systemics, as soil drenches.

Red spider mites. These are serious pests, particularly as the early stages are hard to spot, since the individual mites can barely be seen. Affected leaves become pallid due to the thousands of bleached spots where the mites are feeding on the under surface. The mites are straw-coloured, turning in autumn to minute red spider-like creatures that can clearly be seen with a hand lens, weaving webs over the lower surfaces of the leaves. This pest revels in a hot dry atmosphere and spraying the under surfaces of the leaves of woody plants with water in warm weather helps to prevent trouble. The plants most likely to be attacked are shrubs and carnations, but almost all greenhouse plants are susceptible.

Red spider mites quickly become resistant to any chemical that is used regularly but some reduction of infestations may be obtained by spraying thoroughly with derris, pirimiphos-methyl, malathion or dimethoate.

Alternatively, biological control may be attempted during the summer by introducing the red spider mite predator, *Phytoseiulus persimilis* (for suppliers see opposite).

Glasshouse whitefly. These are tiny snow-white insects that rise into the air when the plants are disturbed. Unfortunately, their larvae are sucking insects with a complicated life cycle and all remedies have to be applied several times to eradicate this persistent pest. Many plants are affected including regal pelargoniums, fuchsias, cucumber, tomato and poinsettia.

Whitefly can be controlled by spraying or fumigating the plants with permethrin. This is a persistent but safe chemical that can be used on a wide range of plants, including tomatoes and cucumbers. Less persistent alternatives are bioresmethrin, pyrethrum, HCH, malathion and pirimiphos-methyl. In some areas there are strains of whitefly that have gained resistance to some of these insecticides.

Biological control may be attempted using a parasite, *Encarsia formosa*, but it only operates effectively above 21°C (70°F).

Aphids. Various forms of greenfly, which may also be buff or pink are certain to appear. Many are killed by any kind of pesticide, but unfortunately some have developed resistance to certain chemicals. I try pyrethrum and derris mixtures before more toxic alternatives. Fully and partially systemic insecticides such as dimethoate, heptenophos and pirimicarb are absorbed into the plant's sap and kill the aphids as they feed. As with all insecticides, the manufacturer's instructions regarding the interval required between spraying and harvesting must be observed if these insecticides are used on food plants. In summer various forms of hover fly take a high toll of green fly and should never be discouraged.

Ants. Ants transport aphids from plant to plant and thereby spread virus diseases as well as pests. For this reason they must be discouraged from establishing themselves in the greenhouse.

HCH dusts or proprietary ant baits may be used in areas where they are troublesome, and these control measures should be applied in and around the nesting sites rather than on plants which ants are visiting.

Earwigs. It is in hot dry summers that earwigs often cause mysterious punctured holes to appear in the leaves of succulents and they also damage chrysanthemum and other flowers.

They can be trapped under old sacking and seed-boxes or in flower pots stuffed with straw or similar materials. HCH dust applied to their hiding places also reduces numbers.

Scales. The protective coverings of scale insects are sometimes found on the backs of the leaves of oleanders and other evergreens. From this safe hiding place they suck the sap of shrubby plants.

Thorough spraying of the undersides of leaves with malathion or nicotine in spring and summer will check infestations, and small pot plants can be hand cleaned using soft rags dipped in soapy water.

Thrips. Thrips are minute blackish grey, winged insects that are hard to find, but the damage they cause is rather similar to that of red spider. They will not become established unless the atmosphere is too dry and spraying with clear water discourages them. If an insecticide is necessary, they can be controlled by spraying with malathion, derris or HCH.

Suppliers of biological predators:

Bunting and Sons, Biological Control, The Nurseries, Great Horkesley, Colchester, Essex

English Woodlands Ltd., Graffham, Petworth, Sussex

H R Thrussell, Pike Plant Products, Antwerp Cottage, Mankinoles, Todmorden, Lancs., OL14 6HR

Natural Pest Control (Amateur), Watermead, Yapton Road, Barnham, Bognor Regis, West Sussex, PO22 0BQ

Nolanvale Ltd., 31 Springfield Road, Bury St. Edmunds, Suffolk

Diseases

Damping-off. This disease is caused by several different soil and water-borne fungi which cause the collapse of seedlings at ground level. It is most troublesome where seedlings are overcrowded, overwatered, or grown in unsterilized compost or watered with water from a dirty tank or butt. Prevent infection therefore, by sowing seeds in sterilized compost and by watering carefully with clean water.

Foot rot, Crown rot and Root rot. May be caused by the same fungi as those causing damping-off and also by others. These organisms cause a brown or black rot of the tissues at the base of the stems, around the crowns or at the roots resulting in wilting or collapse of the top growth. Use sterilized compost and pots and clean water to prevent infection. It is sometimes possible to save a diseased plant by watering with a solution of cheshunt compound or zineb.

Grey mould (Botrytis cinerea). This fungus causes rotting of leaves, stems and flowers, the affected tissues becoming covered with a grey-brown mass of fungal spores. In less severe cases small red or brown spots develop on petals. The disease is most troublesome in greenhouses where the humidity is high and hygiene is poor. Prevent infection by the prompt removal and burning of all diseased or dying parts. Ventilate well to reduce the humidity and water early in the morning and not at night. Fumigate with tecnazene smokes, or spray with captan, carbendazim, benomyl or thiophanate-methyl at the first signs of the disease.

Powdery mildew. This type of disease shows as a white powdery coating on the leaves and sometimes the flowers and the stems of chrysanthemums, begonias, cinerarias and occasionally other plants. As the fungi are encouraged by humid atmospheres ventilate the greenhouse well. Plants that are dry at the roots are more susceptible to infection so water before the compost dries out completely. Remove severely affected leaves and spray with benomyl, carbendazim, dinocap, propiconazole, pyrazophos, thiophanate-methyl or triforine.

Rusts. The rusts of fuchsias and cineraria show as orange powdery pustules on the lower leaf surfaces, but on chrysanthemums, pelargoniums and carnations the pustules produce masses of chocolate-coloured spores. Remove and burn affected leaves and in severe cases destroy the whole plant. Ventilate the greenhouse well to reduce the humidity, and when watering, make sure that droplets do not remain on the leaves. Spray at seven to ten-day intervals with mancozeb or zineb.

Viruses. Cucumber mosaic and other viruses can affect a wide range of plants causing mottling, blotching or striping of the leaves, the affected parts being pale green, yellow or black. The leaves may also be distorted and the plants stunted. Destroy any plant showing these symptoms. Control aphids by suitable spraying as these pests transmit some viruses including cucumber mosaic.

Physiological disorders. These are due to unsuitable cultural conditions and are very common on greenhouse plants. The commonest disorder is called Oedema and in this the plant shows pale pimple-like outgrowths on the undersurface of the leaves and on the stems. Later they burst and become brown and powdery or corky. Ivy-leaved pelargoniums are particularly susceptible to this trouble which is due to overwatering and/or too humid an atmosphere. Improve the cultural conditions by careful watering and ventilation. Do not remove affected leaves.

Bud drop. The dropping or withering of buds is usually due to drying out of the compost at a critical stage of growth. Do not allow the compost to dry out when flower buds are just beginning to develop.

Corky scab of cacti shows as irregular rusty or corky spots which develop into sunken patches. This is due to lack of light and too high humidity or by over-exposure to sunlight. Where the trouble is very unsightly propagate from the affected plant and give the new plants correct cultural treatment.

As temperatures fall in the autumn it becomes especially important to remove dead flowers and foliage and to avoid a damp and stuffy atmosphere. Moulds develop most easily on decayed vegetation, but flowers and soft growth may be spoiled by the dreaded grey mould (see above) if there is not heat or ventilation to keep the air moving.

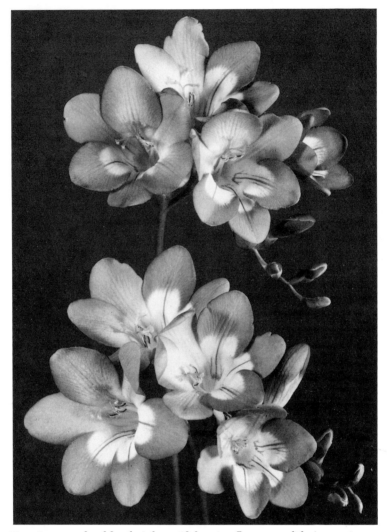

Freesias are valued for their beautiful spring flowers and their sweet scent.

For those who do not use a greenhouse in winter this is the time to take out and burn all those plant remains, while the rest of us make the hard decisions as to what to save and what to propagate for another year. By late September we need to be ready for a hard frost with all tender plants under cover, the heating system tested, and fuel in store. For the real greenhouse enthusiast there are flowers for every season and the warmer the greenhouse the earlier our spring.